WILDLIFE OF NORTH AMERICA

# The Armadillo

## by Steve Potts

**Content Consultant:**
James Taulman
Department of Biological Sciences
University of Arkansas

CAPSTONE PRESS
MANKATO, MINNESOTA

C A P S T O N E     P R E S S

818 North Willow Street • Mankato, Minnesota 56001

http://www.capstone-press.com

Printed in the United States of America.

*Library of Congress Cataloging-in-Publication Data*
Potts, Steve, 1956-
    The armadillo /by Steve Potts.
    p. cm.--(Wildlife of North America)
    Includes bibliographical references (p. 44) and index.
    Summary: Details the characteristics, habitats, and life cycle of the nine-
banded armadillo.
    ISBN 1-56065-545-3
    1. Nine-banded armadillo--Juvenile literature.
[1. Nine-banded armadillo. 2. Armadillos.]    I. Title. II. Series.
QL737.E23P68   1998
599.3'12--dc21

                                              97-5962
                                               CIP
                                                AC

Photo credits
Jeff Foott, 8, 10, 12, 17, 20, 22, 25, 26, 35, 36, 43
Charles Melton, 14, 38-39, 40-41
Dan Polin, 30
Leonard Lee Rue III, 28
Unicorn Stock/Russell Grundke, 6; Bernard Hehl, 18
Lynn M. Stone, cover

# Table of Contents

*Fast Facts about Armadillos* .............................. 4

*Chapter 1* The Armadillo .............................. 7

*Chapter 2* Survival .............................. 13

*Chapter 3* Armadillo Life .............................. 21

*Chapter 4* Past and Future .............................. 31

Photo Diagram .............................. 40

Words to Know .............................. 42

To Learn More .............................. 44

Useful Addresses .............................. 45

Internet Sites .............................. 46

Index .............................. 48

# Fast Facts about Armadillos

**Scientific Name:** *Dasypus novemcinctus*

**Length:** An average adult armadillo is about two and one-half feet (75 centimeters) long including its tail.

**Weight:** Armadillos generally weigh between nine and 16 pounds (four and seven kilograms).

**Physical Features:** A protective outer shell covers an armadillo's body. It is called a carapace and is hard like armor. The carapace is usually brown.

**Habits:** Armadillos are shy, nocturnal animals. Nocturnal means active at night. They can jump up to two feet (60 centimeters) into the air when they are frightened.

**Color:** Armadillos can be different colors. Some armadillos are greenish. Others are black. Some are dark brown or gray.

**Food:** Armadillos eat insects and plants. Their main food is beetles.

**Reproduction:** Armadillos mate between late June and September. A newborn armadillo is called a pup. Pups are usually born between February and May. Female armadillos always give birth to quadruplets. Quadruplets are four identical armadillo pups.

**Life span:** Armadillos can live from seven to 10 years. Pet armadillos have lived for up to 16 years.

**Range:** Armadillos live in South America, Central America, and the southern United States.

**Habitat:** Most armadillos live in warm places with a lot of rainfall. They prefer living in wooded areas with loose, sandy soil. Armadillos often build their homes by ponds or streams.

# Chapter 1

# The Armadillo

There are many kinds of armadillo. The nine-banded armadillo is the only kind that lives in North America. It lives in the southern United States. It also lives in parts of Central America and South America. Other kinds of armadillos live only in South America.

Armadillos are mammals. This means they are warm-blooded animals with a backbone. Mammals give birth to live young. Young mammals nurse from their mothers.

## Armadillo Bands

The nine-banded armadillo received its name from the bands that circle its body. The bands are

The nine-banded armadillo lives in North America.

Its nine bands help an armadillo stretch and twist.

made of tough skin. Usually, the nine-banded armadillo has nine bands. Sometimes it has as few as eight bands or as many as 11 bands.

Bands help the armadillo. They protect it from enemy attacks. The bands help give an armadillo flexibility. Flexibility means being able to bend. In between the bands, the armadillo has skin and strong muscles. The muscles help the armadillo stretch and twist.

8

## Armadillo Appearance

The armadillo has an unusual appearance. Many people have a hard time deciding what kind of animal the armadillo is. Parts of the armadillo look like several other animals. The famous scientist John Audubon said that the armadillo looked like a small pig in a turtle's shell.

Both male and female armadillos look the same. They both have a thick outer skin. This outer skin is called a carapace. It protects armadillos like armor.

Carapaces make armadillos very sensitive to weather. Armadillos lose a lot of body heat through their carapaces. The carapaces are hard-skin shells that are not covered by fur. Armadillos can only live in warm areas because of this.

Armadillos have small heads. Their eyes are small. They have long snouts. Their ears are large and pointed at the ends. They have claws that grow up to one and one-half inches (almost four centimeters) long.

Armadillos have long tails. Twelve to 14 bony rings cover the tails. Often their tails are

half as long as their bodies. Their tails usually grow from nine to 15 inches (23 to 38 centimeters) long.

Armadillos can be different colors. Some armadillos are greenish. Others are black. Some are dark brown or gray. Their color helps them blend into their surroundings. It is often hard to see armadillos. This helps protect armadillos against enemies.

The average armadillo is about the size of a large cat. It is usually two and one-half feet (75 centimeters) long including its tail. Fully grown armadillos weigh between nine and 16 pounds (four and seven kilograms).

## Armadillo Senses

Armadillos cannot see well. They cannot hear well either. Because these senses are so weak, armadillos rely on their keen sense of smell.

Each armadillo has its own scent. Armadillos recognize other armadillos by their scents. Scents also help armadillos sense danger. They can smell other animals or humans. Sometimes armadillos rise on their back legs to sniff the air.

Armadillos use scents to find food, too. They can smell small insects and plants that are up to seven inches (18 centimeters) below the ground.

# Chapter 2

# Survival

Most animals have ways of protecting themselves against their enemies. The armadillo does, too. The armadillo's carapace helps keep it safe. The carapace looks like brown armor. Spanish explorers who found the armadillo named it "little armored animal."

The carapace protects the armadillo while it looks for food. The armadillo can squeeze past sharp objects. It pushes over brush and grass with its armor. Still, not all of the armadillo is protected. Its stomach, the tip of its nose, and the skin between its bands are not covered by the carapace. The armadillo's armor only covers its back, legs, head, and tail.

An armadillo's carapace does not cover the tip of its nose.

An armadillo can dig a hole in two minutes.

### Reacting to Danger

Some kinds of armadillos roll up in a ball when they are in danger. The nine-banded armadillo does not.

When surprised, the nine-banded armadillo rises on its hind feet. It uses its tail to balance as it sways back and forth. It sniffs the air with its nose. The armadillo can smell an enemy. If that happens, the armadillo begins to run.

14

When frightened, the nine-banded armadillo leaps into the air. Often it will jump one to two feet (30 to 60 centimeters) off the ground. When it lands, the armadillo begins to run. Because armadillos jump when frightened, many are often hit by cars.

**Defense**

Armadillos do not have many natural enemies. Only cougars regularly eat armadillos. Even so, armadillos usually avoid fights. They defend themselves by running away. They run into an area of thick brush. Most enemies cannot follow them there. Armadillos can run very fast. They can even outrun humans over short distances.

Sometimes armadillos cannot outrun their enemies. Then they use their claws to dig to safety. Their carapaces protect their backs from enemies while they dig. In two minutes, armadillos can dig holes large enough for hiding. It is almost impossible for enemies to remove armadillos from their holes. Once they are in their holes, they are safe.

Armadillos usually use their claws to help them gather food. But sometimes armadillos use their claws for protection. Armadillos can scratch enemies if they are attacked.

### Swimming

Most types of armadillos can swim when necessary. They swim in order to escape from their enemies. They swim to protect themselves from floods, too.

Nine-banded armadillos swim by breathing in a lot of air. This inflates their stomachs and intestines. The air helps armadillos float. Then they use their legs to paddle across the water.

Most armadillos can swim underwater, too. They take a deep breath and hold it. They let themselves drop underwater. Then they walk on the bottom of a river or pond. Most armadillos can stay underwater for up to eight minutes.

### Foods

Armadillos eat both plants and insects. Their main food is beetles. They also eat berries and

roots. Sometimes they eat small frogs, toads, snakes, crayfish, and shrimp. But they only eat these things if they can catch them easily.

Armadillos eat fire ants, too. Fire ants came to the United States from South America. Fire ants have a bite that is very painful to humans. Armadillos help prevent the spread of fire ants in the United States. Armadillos also eat insects that could damage farmers' crops.

Armadillos dig furrows in the ground to find food.

### Finding Food

Armadillos need large areas to hunt for food. On an average night, armadillos will roam from five to 10 acres (two to four hectares) to look for something to eat.

Armadillos' long snouts help them find food. They put their snouts into the ground and move forward. This digs a furrow three to four inches (eight to 10 centimeters) deep. A furrow is a small channel made in soil.

Armadillos smell the ground as they make furrows. If they smell food, they use their claws to dig deeper holes. They dig until they uncover the hidden insects or plants.

Armadillos also make little round holes in piles of leaves and brush in the woods. These holes are signs that armadillos have been there looking for food.

Armadillos use their tongues to catch food. Their tongues are several inches (many centimeters) long and are very sticky. They also have small bumps on them. Eggs or insects stick to the small, gummy bumps. Armadillos' tongues can capture 50 to 60 insects at one time.

Armadillos' teeth are small and not very sharp. Armadillos do not chew their food or bite with their teeth. They only have molars. Molars are broad, flat teeth used to grind food. Armadillos use their molars to crush food.

# Chapter 3

# Armadillo Life

Armadillos usually live peaceful lives in holes in the ground. These holes are called burrows. Burrows protect armadillos from other animals and humans. Burrows keep armadillos cool in summer and warm during winter. Armadillos spend most of their time searching for food.

**Burrows**
Most armadillos live by themselves. But occasionally scientists have found three or four armadillos in the same burrow. Each armadillo usually makes four or five burrows. One burrow is their home. They hide in the other burrows when they are in danger.

Armadillos live in holes called burrows.

Armadillos spend a lot of time digging their burrows. Sometimes they dig them under the edges of mud banks or ledges. Armadillos prefer soft, sandy soil. This is because soft ground is easier to dig out for their burrows.

Armadillos also try to dig their burrows in high ground. High ground is land that is raised like hills. This helps armadillos escape from water when it rains hard. If too much water gets into their burrows, armadillos may drown.

Even so, armadillos try to build their burrows close to a stream or pond. They find insects and other food near water. They often roll around in the mud to cool down. They take baths in the water, too.

Armadillos stay in their burrows during the day. They need to protect themselves from daytime heat. Armadillos are nocturnal animals. This means

ARMADILLO TRACKS

FRONT FOOT

BACK FOOT

Armadillos often roll around in the mud to cool down.

they sleep in the daytime and are active at night. They leave their underground homes to look for food at night.

Armadillos' behavior changes during cold weather. Then armadillos become diurnal. Diurnal means active during the day. In winter, armadillos stay in their burrows to keep warm at night. They only leave during the warmest parts of the day. Adult armadillos can live up to two weeks without eating. Young armadillos can only live one week without eating.

## Making Burrows

Armadillos dig tunnels that are 10 to 15 feet (three to four and one-half meters) long. Usually, the entrances to tunnels are next to large rocks or tree stumps.

The tunnels go underground. Armadillo burrows may be up to five feet (one and one-half meters) underground. Armadillos take deep breaths when they go underground to dig their burrows. They hold their breath while they are digging.

Armadillos hold their breath while they are digging.

24

**Pups are usually born between February and May.**

Armadillos make their nests at the end of the tunnels. The nests are wider than the tunnels. Armadillos sleep in their nests. They line the nests with grass and leaves.

Armadillos collect nesting material in an interesting way. They use their feet and legs to pick up grass and leaves. They hold this nesting material to their stomachs with their front legs. Then they hop backward toward their burrows. Armadillos use more nesting material than most other animals. The grass and leaves keep armadillos warm and dry.

## Mating

Armadillos have one mate during each breeding season. They do not mate for life. Females are at least one year old before they mate.

Usually, armadillos mate between late June and September. After mating, males leave. Females are responsible for giving birth and raising the newborn armadillos. Young armadillos are called pups.

After mating, female armadillos make nests for their pups. They press down the leaves and grass in the nests. Then the nests are ready for pups.

Eight months after mating, females give birth. Pups are usually born between February and May.

## Armadillo Pups

Female armadillos usually give birth to quadruplet pups. Quadruplets are four identical newborns of the same sex.

Armadillo pups are much more active than many other newborn animals. They open their eyes and walk within hours of their birth.

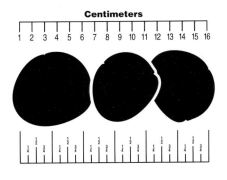

Centimeters

Pups drink their mothers' milk to grow and become stronger. They usually stay in their nests for two to three months. They spend these months growing stronger and sleeping. After that, they are large enough to survive outside.

Newborn pups have very soft and shiny skin. Their carapaces are pale pink. Within days, their skin begins to harden. Their pink shells turn brown or gray. When pups leave the nest, their carapaces are strong enough to protect them.

In their natural surroundings, average armadillos live from seven to 10 years. Pet armadillos have lived for up to 16 years.

Armadillo pups leave their nest after two to three months.

# Chapter 4

# Past and Future

The armadillo has existed for thousands of years. The Mayan people tell a story that describes why the armadillo was created. Mayans are Native American people. They live in Mexico and Central America.

Once, the Mayan gods were having problems. There were two gods who were not acting the right way. Hachakyum (Hah-ah-KYUM) was the Mayan Sun God. He was more powerful than the two misbehaving gods. He decided to teach them a lesson.

Hachakyum called all the Mayan gods together. He made the two misbehaving gods sit together on a bench.

Armadillos have existed for thousands of years.

Hachakyum then turned the bench into a pair of armadillos. The armadillos became frightened and jumped in the air. The two misbehaving gods tumbled to the ground. The fall embarrassed them in front of the other gods.

### History of Armadillos
Some scientists believe that the armadillo came from the glyptodont. The glyptodont was a large dinosaur that was similar to the armadillo.

Armadillos lived in the United States, Central America, and South America thousands of years ago. But the armadillos in the United States mysteriously died. Scientists believe armadillos died because the weather became unusually cold. In the 1800s, armadillos began returning to the United States. They moved up from Central America.

### Increasing Range of Armadillos
Armadillos' range in the United States is increasing. Armadillos are quickly moving into new areas. Their range increases about two and one-half to six and one-half miles (four to 10

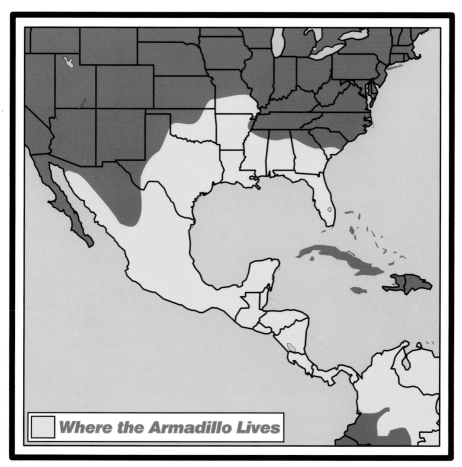

**Where the Armadillo Lives**

kilometers) every year.

Scientists have learned that armadillos can live in places that have fewer than 24 days below freezing every year. Areas must also receive 15 inches (38 centimeters) of rain every year. Many areas in the United States have these conditions. Every year, armadillos spread into more of these areas.

Humans have helped spread armadillos, too. Humans have moved armadillos to new areas where they did not live before. This is called translocation. If the conditions are right, armadillos will survive and mate. Translocation introduced armadillo populations to Florida, Louisiana, Mississippi, and Alabama.

## Dangers to Armadillos

Armadillo populations still face many dangers. The weather is a big danger. Armadillos do not have fur to keep them warm. They stay in their burrows to help them keep warm. They will die if the temperature is too cold.

Armadillos cannot store very much water in their bodies. They also die when there is a drought. A drought is a long period of no rain.

Armadillos have a hard time escaping from humans. Armadillos like to hunt for food and dig burrows in people's lawns, parks, and

An armadillo does not have fur to keep it warm.

**Armadillos often walk across highways to look for food.**

gardens. This can cause a lot of damage. So humans often try to kill armadillos.

People also like to eat armadillos. During the 1930s, many people in the South ate armadillos when they could not find any other food. Some people in Texas called armadillos the poor man's pigs. This is because armadillo meat tastes like pork. Some people in the South still eat armadillo meat.

Cars are another danger to armadillos. Armadillos often walk across highways to find food at night. The bright lights from the cars attract insects that armadillos eat. When the armadillo is scared by a car, it jumps into the air. The car hits the armadillo and kills it. Every year, thousands of armadillos are killed along roads.

## Armadillos and Leprosy

People use armadillos to help them learn about leprosy (LEP-ruh-see). Leprosy is a disease that attacks the skin, nerves, and muscles. Leprosy often paralyzes affected body parts. Paralyzed means unable to function. Someday, armadillos might help scientists find a cure for leprosy.

Armadillos are the only animals besides humans that can become infected with leprosy. Plus, armadillos with leprosy cannot pass the disease along to humans. Scientists have studied leprosy in armadillos. This has helped scientists develop a way to prevent leprosy. By studying armadillos, scientists also hope to discover a cure.

An armadillo is a shy animal.

### Armadillos and the Future

Scientists believe that 30 to 60 million armadillos live in the southern United States today. But people rarely see a live armadillo. They are very shy, nocturnal animals. Sometimes their strange

tracks are the only sign of armadillos. Armadillos leave four footprints and a long line where they have dragged their tails.

Armadillos are continuing to spread into many areas of North America. Despite many dangers, armadillo populations are doing well.

**Snout**

**Nine Bands**

**Carapace**

**Ringed Tail**

**Claws**

# Words to Know

**burrow** (BUR-oh)—a tunnel or hole in the ground that is made and used by an animal for a home

**carapace** (KAR-ah-payss)—thick, protective shell that covers most of the armadillo

**diurnal** (dye-UR-nuhl)—active during the day

**drought** (DROUT)—a long period of no rain

**furrow** (FUR-oh)—a small channel made in soil

**leprosy** (LEP-ruh-see)—a disease that attacks the skin, nerves, and muscles; body parts affected by leprosy often become paralyzed

**Mayans** (MEYE-ahnss)—Native Americans who lived in Mexico and Central America hundreds of years ago

**molar** (MOH-lur)—a broad, flat tooth used for grinding food

**nocturnal** (nok-TUR-nuhl)—active at night

**translocation** (transs-loh-KAY-shuhn)—human introduction of an animal to a new area

An armadillo's carapace does not cover its stomach.

# To Learn More

**Blassingame, Wyatt**. *The Strange Armadillo.*
New York: Dodd Mead, 1983.

**Lavies, Bianca**. *It's an Armadillo!* New York:
E.P. Dutton, 1989.

**Smith, Larry L. and Robin W. Doughty**. *The
Amazing Armadillo: Geography of a Folk
Critter.* Austin, Tex.: University of Texas
Press, 1984.

**Stuart, Dee**. *The Astonishing Armadillo.*
Minneapolis: Carolrhoda Books, 1993.

# Useful Addresses

**Defenders of Wildlife**
1101 14th Street NW
Suite 1400
Washington, DC 20005

**National Wildlife Federation**
1400 16th Street NW
Washington, DC 20036-2217

**Texas Parks and Wildlife Foundation**
4200 Smith School Road
Austin, TX 78744

**U.S. Fish and Wildlife Service**
1849 C Street NW
Washington, DC 20240

# Internet Sites

**Armadillo Online**
http://pilot.msu.edu/user/nixonjos/index.htm

**The Electronic Zoo**
http://netvet.wustl.edu/e-zoo.htm

**ZooNet**
http://www.mindspring.com/~zoonet

Armadillos use their claws to dig.

# Index

Audubon, John, 9

bands, 7, 8, 13
burrow, 21, 23, 24, 34

car, 15, 37
carapace, 4, 9, 13, 29
claws, 9, 15, 16, 19
color, 4, 10

diurnal, 24
drought, 34

fire ants, 17
food, 5, 13, 16, 18, 21, 24
furrow, 18, 19

glyptodont, 32

jump, 4, 15, 32, 37

leprosy, 37

mammal, 7
mating, 5, 27
Mayans, 31

nest, 26, 27, 29
nocturnal, 4, 23, 38

pup, 5, 27, 29

quadruplets, 5, 27

range, 5, 32

smell, 11, 14, 19
snout, 9, 18
swimming, 16

tail, 9, 10, 13, 14
teeth, 19
Texas, 36
tongue, 19
translocation, 34
tunnel, 24